NATIONAL GEOGRAPHIC

T0045237

How Are Magnets Used?

Jan Pritchett

Magnets

Magnets are used for lots of different things.
Magnets can stick to some metals.
They can be used to stick, or hold, things together.
Magnets are used all around us.

MAGNETS

Game Boards

This checkerboard is made of metal.
There is a magnet in each checker.
The magnets in the checkers stick to the board.
The magnets keep the checkers from falling off the board.

Refrigerator Doors

To keep things cold, a refrigerator door must close tightly.
There is a magnetic strip around the door.
The magnetic strip sticks to the metal frame of the refrigerator.
The magnet keeps the door closed tightly.

Message Boards

A message board holds information for people to read. The message board is made of metal.

Magnets stick to the metal board. The magnets hold the papers in place.

Games Day
CROSS STREET SCHOOL

Toy Trains

This toy train has cars that move together.
Each train car has a magnet at the front and the back.
The magnets stick to each other.
The magnets keep the train cars together.

How else do you use magnets?